I0472559

The New Earth Series Presents

Quantitative Decision-Making for Business Analysis

By

Dr. Enid Alane Thompson

Published by CreateSpace Self-Publishing (LLC), an Amazon Company, and Kindle

Direct Publishing (LLC) Copyright of Book is held by the Author.

2016

Preface

Dear Reader,

Business analytics (BA) is the practice of iterative, methodical exploration of an organization's data with emphasis on statistical analysis. Business analytics is designed for leaders committed to data-driven decision making. I provide examples of various test utilizing discriminant analysis, ANOVA, t-Test, and others to help you understand how statistics can be learned and implemented for making sound business decisions.

Dedication

All my work is dedicated to my family, friends, and for anyone who desires to make a positive change in the world.

Table of Contents

Introduction

How would you align your thought process with an integrative model?

An integrative model is a learning tool with three benefits for the individual new to the research process, the novice researcher. The three benefits include:

- Saving the individual time and money

- Provides a central picture for the research design using statistical tools

- Provides the individual the ability to evaluate which empirical data would support specific business decisions.

The integrative model process supports various area of research for the business minded individual (i.e., builds knowledge, formulate hypotheses, develop measures, would help select the best analytical technique, and data collection) responsible for organizational decision-making. The integrative model supported my research study entitled "*Managing Effective Communication after a Crisis.*" The purpose of my research was to explore the role of crisis communication, planning, and the **leader decision-making** process after a crisis. A variety of quantitative research like (Mann, 2014, Khan, 2013, Ruggiero, 2013) discovered a direct correlation between crisis communication and the recovery efforts of large companies during and after a crisis or catastrophic event. These published studies align with Corner's (2002) notes regarding exercises illustrating the integrative model. To fill in the gaps or further the continuum in research while aligning the business decision-making processes with the model, would entail asking a question about the relationships among certain variables (Creswell, 2013). The research question(s) would look something like this:

Research Questions:

1. What is the correlation between a company's size and the effectiveness of its crisis communication planning and effective communication after the crisis?

2. What is the correlation between a company's size and the propensity to develop and implement successful strategies for crisis communication and recovery efforts?

Hypotheses:

- H1: Large companies are less likely to influence crisis communication responses for competitive opportunities and quick recovery after a crisis.

- H2: Small companies are less likely to develop strategic plans for crisis communications than large companies are.

In this book, I provide several examples that will help you understand how to use SPSS as a tool to support methodical exploration of an organization's data with emphasis on statistical analysis for decision-making. First, let us look at the impact of designing experiments.

Designing Experiments

The basic intent of an experimental design is to test the impact of a treatment on an outcome, controlling for all other factors that might influence that outcome (Campbell, 2010). As one form of control, researchers randomly assign individuals to groups. When one receives a treatment and the other group does not, the experimenter can isolate whether if it is the treatment and not other factors that influence the outcome (Creswell,

2013). Both true experimental design and quasi-experiments have similarities as well as differences.

Similarities between true and quasi-experiments:

(a) Study participants are subjected to some type of treatment or condition

(b) Some outcome of interest is measured

(c) The researchers test whether differences in this outcome are related to the treatment

Differences between true experiments and quasi-experiments:

(1) In a true experiment, participants are randomly assigned to either the treatment or the control group, whereas they are not assigned randomly in a quasi-experiment.

(2) In a quasi-experiment, the control and treatment groups differ not only in terms of the experimental treatment they receive, but also in other, often unknown or unknowable, ways. Thus, the researcher must try to statistically control for as many of these differences as possible.

(3) Because control is lacking in quasi-experiments, there may be several "rival hypotheses" competing with the experimental manipulation as explanations for observed results.

Research Question

What is the significant relationship between the safety climate, the number of employees in an area/team managed by the supervisor and the injury rate after a crisis?

Hypothesis

HO (null) there is no significant relationship between the safety climate, number of employees in an area/team managed by the supervisor and the injury rate after a crisis.

H1 (alternate) there is a significant relationship between the safety climate, number of employees in an area/team managed by the supervisor and the injury rate after a crisis.

How might you design an experiment that will effectively collect data for this chosen hypothesis?

To collect data for this quasi-experimental design for the safety climate, use the average number of employees with the perception of the supervisor's priority for safety and health over a 12-month period. Observers will measure the climate 4 times during the 12-month period. For the number of hours worked use the number of actual hours worked by all employees in the area/team for the 12-month period ending 12/31/2009. Finally, for the injury rate use the average rate of injuries per 100 employees over the 12-month period.

How will you minimize threats to validity?

Internal validity is the basic minimum without which any experiment is uninterpretable. External validity centers on generalizability. For example, to what population, setting, treatment variables, and measurement variables can this effect be generalized? To minimize threats to validity the researcher must use adequate definitions and measures of variables. In addition, identify any potential threats to validity that may arise in the study. The researcher may need to incorporate a separate section in the proposal to advance the threat.

Will it be a true experiment or a quasi-experiment?

For the hypotheses noted above the best design is quasi-experimental. The quasi-experiment participants are subjected to some type of treatment or condition. In addition, some outcome of interest is measured and the researcher will test whether differences in this outcome are related to the treatment. Moreover, because control is lacking in quasi-experiments, there may be several "rival hypotheses" competing with the experimental manipulation as explanations for observed results. Now, let's move into working with SPSS software for statistical analysis.

Chapter 1: Working with SPSS Software (Part 1)

This section outlines the measures for the central tendency of certain variables. The variables include the number of employees, hours worked, safety behavior, injury rate, and safety climate. In addition, we will examine the frequency distributions for the site, supervisor gender, and risk level. The data was gathered from three locations, which included (a) Boston, (b) Phoenix, and (c) Seattle.

Application- Occupational Safety

Occupational safety is an area concerned with the safety, health, and the welfare of people engaged in work or employment (Pinto 2013). Work related injuries cost employers large sums of revenue each year. To combat the high number of injuries on the job, leaders and subordinates must anticipate accidents in the workplace (OSHA, 2014).

Background

The central theme of this section emphases the substantive analysis of the following measures for frequency found in the following nine variables: number of employees, hours worked, safety behavior, injury rate, and safety climate, the site, supervisor gender, and risk level. The central focus is the number of hours worked and how the number of hours worked may contribute to the injury rate at each location.

Research Question

How does the number of hours work contribute to the injury rate?

Hypotheses

HO (null) a significant relationship does not exist between the number of hours worked and the injury rate.

H1 (alternate) a significant relationship does exist between the hour's work and the injury rate.

Coding, Definitions, and Theme Analysis

A part of data analysis and interpretation is the coding process. Coding is the process of organizing the material into chunks or segments of text before bringing (themes) meaning to information. The following codes and definitions were used in this section and will be utilized in future test located in this book to analysis the nine variables.

- **# Emps-   Numbers of employees in the area/team managed by the supervisor**
- **Hours Worked-Number of actual hours worked by all employee in the area/team for the 12 month period ending 12/31/2009**
- **Supervisor Gender-   Male = 0 Female = 1**
- **Percentage (%) of Safe Behavior-Regular observations of employee**

behavior were made over the 12-month period by independent trained, objective observers. This represents the percentage of those behaviors that were deemed to represent safe acts by the observer

- **Injury Rate - Average rate of injuries per 100 employees over the 12-month period**

- **Risk-Operations for supervisors differed regarding activities and risks. Risks ranged from low (1) office-related activities to high (7) manual material handling activities**

- **Safety Climate - Average employee perception of the supervisor's priority for safety and health over the 12-month period. Observers measured climate four times during the 12-month period.**

Descriptive Statistics

Table 1

The number of hours worked in the 15 Boston locations was 705,120 in the 19 Phoenix locations 956,800 and the 17 Seattle locations 886,080. There were fifty-one locations with 47.5% men as supervisors and 52.9% women as supervisors. The average hours worked in each location is approximately 50,000. The rate of injury for all locations carries a standard deviation of 17.47%.

	Min	Max	*M*	*SD*
Number of Employees	5	45	24.02	7.50
Hours Worked	10400	93600	49960.78	15590.24
Percent Safety Behavior	.42%	1.00%	.87%	.14%

Injury Rate	.000	76.92%	15.18%	17.48%
Safety Climate	2.50%	6.80%	4.70%	1.03%
Risk	1%	7%	4.59%	2.01%

Table 2

Frequency Distribution: Site

LOCATION	FREQUENCY	PERCENT
Boston	15	29.4%
Phoenix	19	37.3%
Seattle	17	33.3%
TOTAL		**100.00**

Table 3

Frequency Distribution: Supervisor Gender

	FREQUENCY	PERCENT
Man	24	47.1%
Woman	27	52.9%
TOTAL		**100.00**

Recommendation for Future Research. The need for additional research is warranted. To answer the research question and derive at which hypotheses is true, the researcher must consider the total number of employees at each site, the number of hours worked, the rate of injury among the gender of the supervisors, risk, safe behavior, and safety climate.

The analysis presented in this section is inconclusive; an in-depth analysis is needed to examine the relationship between the number of hours worked, and the injury rate of each location. In addition, the individual must examine the injury rate and the risk level of the safe behavior and safety climate. Human resources management teams and senior management should include strategies that improve the overall safety environment in the workplace. Moreover, conduct training and educational videos to support the advancement of occupational safety.

Chapter 2: Analyzing SPSS (PASW) Software (Part 2)

Background, History, and Objective

This section contains the measures for the central tendency of two certain variables. The two variables were the safety climate and the injury rate. The purpose of the test was to determine if there was a significant relationship between the safety climate and the injury rate in three manufacturing locations. The three locations were Boston, Phoenix, and Seattle. The data was analyzed using SPSS Software and based on guidelines provided by Green and Salkind (2008). The analysis includes a descriptive statistics. The following null hypothesis was tested using regression analysis:

Research Question

What is the significant relationship between the safety climate and the injury rate?

Hypothesis

HO (null) There is no significant relationship between safety climate and injury rate.

H1 (alternate) There is a significant relationship between the safety climate and the injury rate.

An independent, trained, observer that collected the data observed the two variables in the hypothesis. The observer made regular observations of the employee behavior. The average employee perception of the supervisor's priority for safety and health was measured. Observers measured climate safety four times during a 12-month

period ending 12/31/2009. The average rate of injuries per 100 employees over the 12-

month period is shown below. The dependent variable was the Injury Rate and the Safety

Climate. The independent variable was the Site.

Data Analysis

Descriptive Statistics

	N	Range	Mean	Std. Deviation
InjuryRate	51	76.923	15.17570	17.474677
SafetyClimate	51	4.300	4.69706	1.034973

Table 1
Safety Climate and Injury Rate by Site

Site		InjuryRate	SafetyClimate
Boston	Mean	15.62977	3.85267
	N	15	15
	Std. Deviation	13.877108	.789507
Phoenix	Mean	17.17757	5.31105
	N	19	19
	Std. Deviation	21.205157	.977814
Seattle	Mean	12.53765	4.75588
	N	17	17
	Std. Deviation	16.356918	.778830
Total	Mean	15.17570	4.69706
	N	51	51
	Std. Deviation	17.474677	1.034973

Regression Analysis

The results of the regression analysis indicated there was no significant

relationship between the safety climate and the injury rate. The regression analysis

generated F=0.008p= 0.930 indicating that safety climate, as a predictor of injury rate, was not significant since p> 0.05. This is apparent from the line graph, which shows little

correlation between safety climate and injury rate. Moreover, the chart reflects a high

degree of variation suggesting difficulty in predicting mean injury at any point in time.

Figure 1 illustrates *R Squared* and Figure 2 illustrates ANOVA reflecting the P-Value of

930b

Model Summary

Mode l	R	R Square	Adjusted R Square	Std. Error of the Estimate
1	.013[a]	.000	-.020	17.650672

a. Predictors: (Constant), SafetyClimate

ANOVA[a]

Model		Sum of Squares	df	Mean Square	F	Sig.
1	Regression	2.453	1	2.453	.008	.930[b]
	Residual	15265.765	49	311.546		
	Total	15268.217	50			

a. Dependent Variable: InjuryRate

b. Predictors: (Constant), SafetyClimate

Figure 3 - Safety climate (x-axis) by injury rate (y-axis)

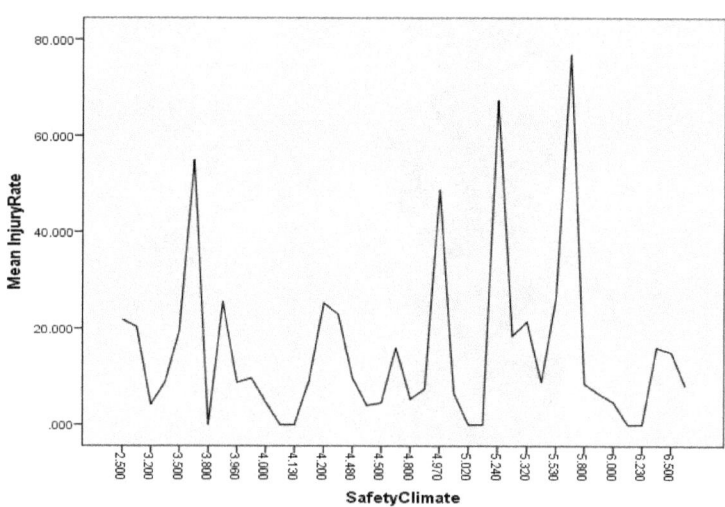

Figure 4 Injury Rate by Site

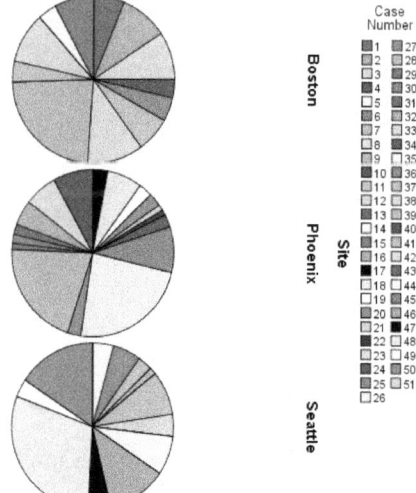

Figure 5 Safety Climate by Site

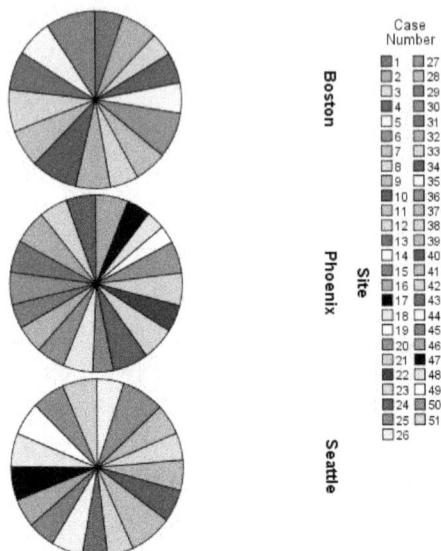

The results indicated that there was no significant relationship between safety

climate and injury rate. Thus, the null hypothesis was rejected. The purpose of the test

was to determine if there was a significant relationship between the safety climate and the

injury rate in three manufacturing locations. The three locations were Boston, Phoenix,

and Seattle.

Chapter 3: Working with SPSS (PASW) Software One-Sample t Test

Green and Salkind (2014) noted that a One-sample t-test assesses whether the

population means on a test variable is different from a constant, called a test value.

Understanding the underlying assumptions for the One-Sample t Test requires knowing

the test variable is normally distributed in the population. In addition, the cases represent

a random sample from the population, and the scores on the test variable are independent

of each other as noted by Green and Salkind.

Purpose of the Test

The purpose of this test was to determine if the *Involvement Technique* of John's new teaching method was effective in teaching algebra to first graders. The researcher randomly sampled all first graders within the Lawrence City School System and taught them individually with the new method. The six students then took an eight-item test; each prescribes four possible answers with each item coded right (1) or wrong (0). This paper contains results of the (a) total scores computed, (b) value test for the problem, (c) and a One-Sample t-Test on the total scores (which include Mean Algebra score, *t*-Test Value, and *p*-Value).

Research Question

Is John's new Algebra teaching method effective?

Hypotheses

H1₀: There is no significant difference between John's new Algebra teaching method than the old teaching method.

H1ₐ: There is a significant difference between John's new Algebra teaching method than the old teaching method.

Data Set for this Test

The data set selected for this exercise was taken from Lesson 22 Exercise File 1 on the web at http://www.pearsonhighered.com/greensalkindSPSS (this was one of my past course assignments). The test was conducted using the following steps click ANALYZE, click Compare Means and next select One-Sample *t*-Test.

In this exercise, the total scores were summed across all eight items by using the Transform compute variable command. The total scores were: 8, 6, 5, 7, 4, and 6. To determine the test value see the numeric expression: ¼ x 8 = 2. The test value for this problem was the Change Level of Performance on the Test Variable.

One- Sample Test Results

One-Sample Statistics				
	N	Mean	Std. Deviation	Std. Error Mean
TotalS	6	6.00	1.414	.577

Table 1- *One-Sample Statistics*

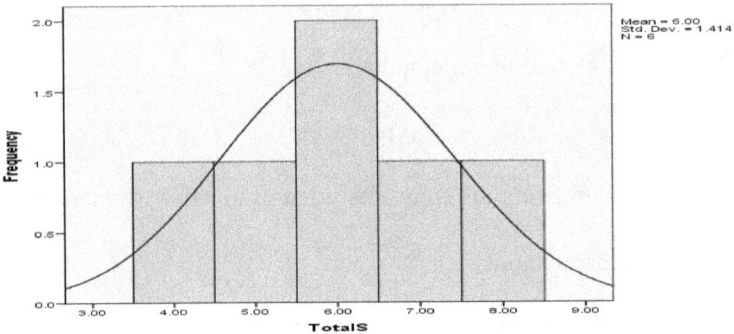

Figure 1- Histogram of frequency of scores

Descriptive Statistics

All students correctly answered Item(s) 1, and 2, one student responded incorrectly to Item(s) 3 and 4; three students responded incorrectly to Item(s) 5; one student responded incorrectly to Item(s) 6; and two students responded incorrectly to Item(s) 7. Four students responded incorrectly to Item(s) 8. The results indicate that the six students had a mean score of 6.00 with a standard deviation of 1.414 Figure 1

illustrates the distribution of scores, indicating that the majority of students scored 70%

or higher.

			One-Sample Test			
			Test Value = 2			
	t	df	Sig. (2-tailed)	Mean Difference	95% Confidence Interval of the Difference	
					Lower	Upper
TotalS	6.928	5	.001	4.000	2.52	5.48

Table 2- *One-Sample t-Test*

Inferential Statistics - A One-sample *t*-test was run to determine if the students'

results were significantly higher than a test value of .7, which would indicate their ability

to answer at least 70% of the questions. The Mean = 6.0, the t = 6.93 and the p = <.01.

The results indicate in the null hypothesis that students' mean score was not significantly

higher than .7 the null was rejected, (see Table 2).

The test was to determine if the *Involvement Technique* of John's new teaching

method was effective or not in teaching algebra to first graders. The results from the (a)

total scores computed, (b) value test for the problem, (c) and One-Sample t-Test on the

total scores (which include Mean Algebra Score, *t*-Test Value, and *p*-Value) suggest

John's new Algebra teaching method was rejected, not effective. The Mean = 6.0, the t =

6.93 and the p = <.01. The results indicate that the null H10 There is no significant

difference between John's new Algebra teaching method than the old teaching method

was accepted. The student's mean score was not significantly higher than .7, while a majority of student got Items 1 and 2 correct the overall score for the group of student

score was less than 70%.

Recommendations - The recommendation regarding John's new algebra teaching method

was not to implement the new Involvement Technique.

Paired Samples *t* Test

			One-Sample Test				
				Test Value = 2			
	t	df	Sig. (2-tailed)	Mean Difference	95% Confidence Interval of the Difference		
						Lower	Upper
TotalS	6.928	5	.001	4.000		2.52	5.48

When conducting a Paired-Samples *t*-Test each case must have scored on two

variables as stated by Green and Salkind, 2014. Table 1 above illustrates a One-sample *t*-

test that was run to determine if the students' results were significantly higher than a test

value of .7, which would indicate their ability to answer at least 70% of the questions.

The results indicate that the null hypothesis which was students' mean score was not

significantly higher than .7 the null was rejected, $t(5) = .69, p = .001$.

Hypotheses

$H1_0$: There is no significant difference between John's new Algebra teaching

methods than the old teaching method.

$H1_A$: There is a significant difference between John's new Algebra teaching

methods than the old teaching method.

Purpose of the Test

The purpose of this test was to compute scores to obtain a total Index of Life Stress (ILS) at age 40 and age 60. To obtain an overall score of life stress, sum the interpersonal and occupational stress measures at each age by using SPSS. Using two variables, one for overall life stress at age 40 and one for overall life stress at 60.

Research Question

Is overall life stress different as working women grow older?

Hypotheses

$H1_0$: Overall life stress is significantly different as working women grow older.

$H1_A$: Overall life stress is not significantly different as working women grow older.

Paired Samples Statistics		Mean	N	Std. Deviation	Std. Error Mean
Pair 1	Inter40	151.8444	45	14.48346	2.15907
	Inter60	136.8667	45	9.94896	1.48310

Table 1-*Paried Samples Statistics*

Descriptive Statistic (See Table 1)

A Pair-Samples *t*-Test was conducted to obtain an overall score of life stress, sum the interpersonal and occupational stress measures at each age by using the Transform, Compute Variable option. Two new variables must be used, one for life stress at age 40, and one for overall life stresses at age 60. In Figure 1, the Histogram shows the results. In addition, the paired-samples t-test was conducted to evaluate whether women's life stress declined from age 40 to age 60. The results indicated that the mean overall life stress index at age 40 (M= 151.84, SD = 14.48) was significantly greater than mean overall life

stress index at age 60 (M = 136.87, SD = 9.95, t (44) = 5.82, $p < .01$.

		Paired Samples Test							
			Paired Differences				t	df	Sig. (2-tailed)
		Mean	Std. Deviation	Std. Error Mean	95% Confidence Interval of the Difference				
					Lower	Upper			
Pair 1	Inter40 - Inter60	14.97778	17.26595	2.57386	9.79051	20.16504	5.819	44	.000

Table 2- *Paired- Samples t Test*

Inferential statistics - A test was conducted to see if the overall occupational

stress declines as women get older, while the interpersonal life stress increase or stay the

same. The 95% confidence interval for the mean difference in overall stress between ages

40 and 60 was 9.79 to 20.16. The effect size was moderately large, d = .87. It appears that

most women, overall life stress scores declined over the 20-year period.

Research Question

Does occupational stress decrease in women as they grow older, while

interpersonal life stress increase or stay the same?

Hypotheses

H1$_0$: Occupational stress decreases as women get older.

H1$_A$: Occupational stress does not decrease, as women get older.

Paired Samples Statistics

		Mean	N	Std. Deviation	Std. Error Mean
Pair 1	Occupational life stress at age 40	73.64	45	9.547	1.423
	Occupational life stress at age 60	61.87	45	6.625	.988
Pair 2	Interpersonal life stress at age 40	78.20	45	11.655	1.737
	Interpersonal life stress at age 60	75.00	45	7.711	1.149

Paired Samples Correlations

		N	Correlation	Sig.
Pair 1	Occupational life stress at age 40 & Occupational life stress at age 60	45	-.207	.173
Pair 2	Interpersonal life stress at age 40 & Interpersonal life stress at age 60	45	.005	.974

Paired Samples Test

		Paired Differences					t	df	Sig. (2-tailed)
		Mean	Std. Deviation	Std. Error Mean	95% Confidence Interval of the Difference				
					Lower	Upper			
Pair 1	Occupational life stress at age 40 - Occupational life stress at age 60	11.778	12.696	1.893	7.964	15.592	6.223	44	.000
Pair 2	Interpersonal life stress at	3.200	13.942	2.078	-.989	7.389	1.540	44	.131

age 40 -
Interpersonal
life stress at
age 60

Findings- The results indicated that the Means for Interpersonal life stress at age 40 was 78.20 and the interpersonal life stress at age 60 was 75.00 the difference was 3.20. When the paired-samples test was run the interpersonal life stress at age 40 and age, 60 was 3.20 no change. The two variables did not decrease they remained the same. The t value = 1.54, p-value = .131. The null that occupational stress decreases as women get older was accepted.

The results indicated that there is no significant relationship between the overall life stress at age 40 and overall life stress at age 60. This lack of a relationship indicates that women's interpersonal stress cannot be predicted from a measure of their occupational stress. The results further indicated that the null hypothesis that the overall life stress is significantly different, as working women grow older was rejected. The significant difference between the mean score of interpersonal life stress at age 40 and the mean score of interpersonal life stress at 60 indicate that women tend to be less stressed as they age. Future researchers should determine why the results indicated that there was no significant relationship between the overall life stress at age 40 and overall life stress at age 60.

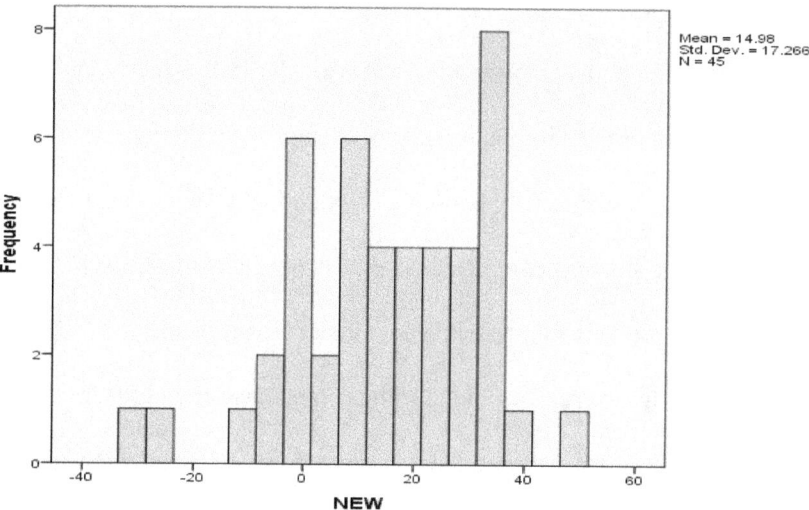

Figure 1 of the Analysis of Exercises 1 through 4 Histogram

Results Section: Analysis of Exercises 1 through 4

Two separate Paired-samples *t*-tests were conducted to evaluate whether the change in life stress from age 40 to age 60 was caused by occupational stress, interpersonal stress or both. The results indicated that interpersonal stress levels did not differ significantly between the two age groups (age 40 and age 60), $t(44) = 1.54, p - .13$, moreover, women's occupational stress decreased significantly during the same period, $t(44) = 6.22, p, .01$. The decline in the overall life stress was primarily a function of the decrease in occupational stress.

Chapter 4: Your Data Interpretation Practicum

The purpose of this section was to determine if John's new teaching method (*Involvement Technique*) is effective in teaching algebra to first graders. In addition, to determine if the test scores of the six students selected were higher than the rest of the 30 first graders tested. The dataset for lesson 22 from week three's application was used to run the descriptive statistics and a One-sample t-test through SPSS, which support the researcher's interpretation of the data. John randomly sampled six first graders from the 30 first grades within the Lawrence City School and individually taught them algebra with the new method. The students completed an eight-item algebra test. Each item describes a problem and presents four possible answers to the problem.

The scores on each item represent (1) for the correct answer and (0) for the incorrect answer. The researcher analyzed the data from lesson 22 week three application using a one- sample t-test to determine if the students' results were significantly higher than a test value of .7, which indicates each students' ability to answer at least 70% of the questions.

Research Question

Is the mean score for the students higher than 70%?

Hypotheses

$H1_0$: The students' mean score is not significantly higher than 70%

$H1_A$: The students' mean score is significantly higher than 70%.

Data Analysis

The test value used for this section was Change Level of Performance on the Test Variable. For the reader to understand the One-Sample t-Test consider the assumptions underlying the test and an associated effect size statistic as used by Green and Salkind, 2008. Next, let us consider that there were two assumptions underlying the One-sample t-test. The first assumption was the test variable is normally distributed in the population.

The second assumption was the case represents a random sample from the population,

and the scores on the test variable are independent of each other.

	Descriptive Statistics			
	N	Mean		Std. Deviation
	Statistic	Statistic	Std. Error	Statistic
item1	6	1.00	.000	.000
item2	6	1.00	.000	.000
item3	6	.83	.167	.408
item4	6	.83	.167	.408
item5	6	.50	.224	.548
item6	6	.83	.167	.408
item7	6	.67	.211	.516
item8	6	.33	.211	.516
SCORE	6	6.0000	.57735	1.41421
Valid N (listwise)	6			

Table 1- The total scores was summed across all eight items by using the Transform

Compute Variable command. The total scores were 8, 6, 5, 7, 4, and 6. To determine the

test value see the numeric expression: ¼ x 8 = 2. To fill in Table 1 SPSS was run by

selecting ANALYZE, DESCRIPTIVES, select Mean, Standard Deviation, and Standard

Error of the Mean.

Findings - Descriptive Statistics

All students correctly answered Item(s) 1 and 2; one student responded

incorrectly to Items 3 and 4; three students responded incorrectly to Item(s) 5; one

student responded incorrectly to Item(s) 6; and two students responded incorrectly to

Item(s) 7. Four students responded incorrectly to Item(s) 8. The results indicate that the

six students had a mean score of 6.00 with a standard deviation of 1.414. Figure 1 illustrates the distribution of scores, indicating that the majority of students did not score

70% or higher.

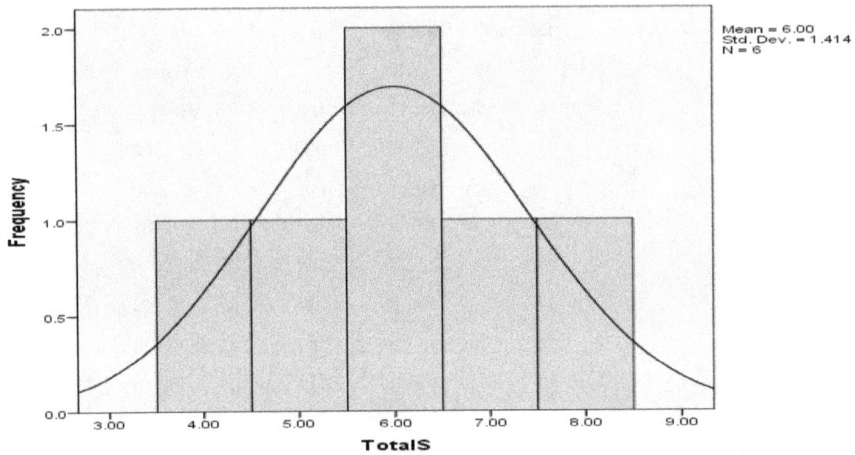

Figure 1 - Histogram of frequency of scores

			One-Sample Test			
			Test Value = 2			
	t	df	Sig. (2-tailed)	Mean Difference	95% Confidence Interval of the Difference	
					Lower	Upper
TotalS	6.928	5	.001	4.000	2.52	5.48

Table 2-*One-Sample t-Test*

Inferential Statistics

      I utilized a one- sample *t*-test to determine if the students' results were

significantly higher than a test value of .7, which would indicate their ability to answer at

least 70% of the questions. The results indicate that the null hypothesis that students'

mean score was not significantly higher than 70% was not rejected. SPSS supplied all the

information necessary to compute an effect size, d given by $d = 4$ and the $SD = 1.414$

where the mean difference and standard deviation was reported in the SPSS output. In addition, the researcher computed d from the t value by using the equation $d = t$ (5) and N = 6 (N is the total sample size), $p = .52$. While a majority of student got Items 1 and 2 correct, the overall score for the group was less than 70%.

The results from the t-test hypothesis $H1_0$: The students' mean score is not significantly higher than 70% was not rejected, the group Mean will not be significantly different. d evaluates the degree that the mean on the test variable differs from the test value in standard deviation units. The results of the One-sample t-test shown above compute a mean and a standard deviation of the test variable. The difference between the Mean value of 6.0 and the test value of 2 is 4. This difference indicates that the students' mean score is not significantly higher than 70%.

Chapter 5: One-Way and Two-Way Analysis of Variance

One-Way ANOVA

The purpose of this study was to determine if there is a significant difference in whether blonde-haired people, brunets, and redhead differ on their extrovertedness. Marvin then administered a measure of social extroversion to each. The measurement of social extroversion was based on a scale of 1 to 10 with 1 being the lower and 10 marking the highest of participants. The study participants consisted of six naturally blond men, six natural burnet men, and six naturally redhead men; all were used for the measurement of the hair color. The test conducted was a one-way ANOVA using SPSS to investigate the relationship between hair color and social extroversion.

In addition, a post hoc test was conducted. The results identified the F ratio for the group effect, Sums of squares for the hair color effect, Means for redheads, and the p-

value for the hair color effect. Moreover, the test results noted the effect size for the relationship between hair color and extroversion. A boxplot was created to display the differences between the distributions for the three hair colors groups.

Research Question

What is the significant difference between the levels of extroversion by hair color?

Hypotheses

$H1_0$ (Null) There is no significant difference in the level of extroversion by hair color.

H1A (Alternate) There is a significant difference in the level of extroversion by hair color.

ANOVA					
Social Extroversion					
	Sum of Squares	df	Mean Square	F	Sig.
Between Groups	24.111	2	12.056	3.511	.056
Within Groups	51.500	15	3.433		
Total	75.611	17			

Table 1 *ANOVA reflecting the Sum of Squares*

Descriptives								
Social Extroversion								
	N	Mean	Std. Deviation	Std. Error	95% Confidence Interval for Mean		Minimum	Maximum
					Lower Bound	Upper Bound		
Blond	6	5.17	2.787	1.138	2.24	8.09	2	10
Brunet	6	3.67	1.211	.494	2.40	4.94	2	5

Redhead	6	2.33	1.033	.422	1.25	3.42	1	4
Total	18	3.72	2.109	.497	2.67	4.77	1	10

Table 2

Descriptive Statistics: Social Extroversion to Hair Color

Descriptive Analysis

The test was run in SPSS selecting ANALYZE, Compare Means, and selecting One-Way
ANOVA. The dependent variable was Social Extroversion and the Factor used was Hair
Color. According to Green and Salkind (2014), the one-way analysis of variance (one-
way ANOVA) must have scores for each or case with two-variables. The two variables
are known as a factor and a dependent variable. The results indicated that the mean and
standard deviation for the level of social extroversion to blond males (M=5.17, SD =
2.79) were higher than the mean and standard deviation for the level of social
extroversion to brunets (M = 3.67, SD = 1.21). The distribution level of social
extroversion for blonde-haired people is between scales of 2 to 10. The distribution level
of social extroversion for burnets is between scales of 2 to 5. The distribution level of
social extroversion for redheads is between scales of 1 to 4. Moreover, the F (2, 15) =
3.51 for the group effect. SS hair color = 24.11 for the Sums of Squares between groups
for the hair color effect. Mean for Redheads = 2.33, the total Mean = 6, and p= .06 for the
hair color effect.

	Social Extroversion			
	Hair Color	N	Subset for alpha = 0.05	
			1	2
Tukey HSD[a]	Redhead	6	2.33	
	Brunet	6	3.67	3.67

	Blond	6		5.17
	Sig.		.446	.365

Means for groups in homogeneous subsets are displayed.

a. Uses Harmonic Mean Sample Size = 6.000.

Figure 1 - Distribution of level of Extroversion by Hair Color

Inferential Statistics

The results of the analysis of variance indicate that there is a significant difference in social extroversion by hair color, F (.446, .365) =.81, p = .06 (see Figure 1 above).

			Multiple Comparisons				
Dependent Variable: Social Extroversion							
	(I) Hair Color	(J) Hair Color	Mean Difference (I-J)	Std. Error	Sig.	95% Confidence Interval	
						Lower Bound	Upper Bound
Tukey HSD	Blond	Brunet	1.500	1.070	.365	-1.28	4.28
		Redhead	2.833*	1.070	.045	.05	5.61
	Brunet	Blond	-1.500	1.070	.365	-4.28	1.28
		Redhead	1.333	1.070	.446	-1.45	4.11
	Redhead	Blond	-2.833*	1.070	.045	-5.61	-.05
		Brunet	-1.333	1.070	.446	-4.11	1.45
Dunnett C	Blond	Brunet	1.500	1.241		-2.54	5.54
		Redhead	2.833	1.213		-1.11	6.78
	Brunet	Blond	-1.500	1.241		-5.54	2.54
		Redhead	1.333	.650		-.78	3.45
	Redhead	Blond	-2.833	1.213		-6.78	1.11
		Brunet	-1.333	.650		-3.45	.78

The mean difference is significant at the 0.05 level.

Table 3

Multiple Comparisons: Effect size for relationship between hair color and social extroversion

The purpose of this test was to determine if there was a significant difference in whether blonde-haired people, brunets, and redhead differ on their extrovertedness. The results identified the F ratio for the group effect, Sums of squares for the hair color effect, Means for redheads, and the p-value for the hair color effect. Moreover, the test results noted the effect size for the relationship between hair color and social extroversion was eat squared $=.32$ which are a moderate effect size. In addition noted the Mean difference was significant at the 0.05 level. Therefore, the hypotheses that there is no significant difference in the level of extroversion by hair color were rejected. The H1A (Alternate) There is a significant difference in the level of extroversion by hair color was Accepted.

Two-way ANOVA

The purpose of the study was to determine how much time fathers of children with a disability played with their children. The researcher conducted a two-way ANOVA to evaluate differences among the groups, according to gender and disability status of the child, in the amount of time fathers spent playing with their children.

Research Question

Is there a significant difference between gender and disability status of the child and the amount of time their fathers play with them?

Hypotheses

H1o (null) There is no significant difference in gender based on the disability status of the child.

H1A (Alternate) There is a significant difference in gender based on the disability status of the child.

33

H1o (null) There is no significant interaction between gender and disability status of the child and the amount of time fathers play with them.

H1A (Alternate) There is a significant interaction between gender and disability status of the child and the amount of time fathers play with them.

Descriptive Statistics				
Dependent Variable: play				
Disability status of the child	Gender of Child	Mean	Std. Deviation	N
Typically Developing	Male	7.30	1.829	10
	Female	6.80	2.201	10
	Total	7.05	1.986	20
Physical Disability	Male	3.00	1.563	10
	Female	3.40	1.897	10
	Total	3.20	1.704	20
Mental Retardation	Male	3.22	1.716	9
	Female	4.00	1.612	11
	Total	3.65	1.663	20
Total	Male	4.55	2.613	29
	Female	4.71	2.369	31
	Total	4.63	2.470	60

Table 4

*Descriptive Statistics: Play Time by Gender and Disability Type (*Above*) and Marginal Means (*Below*)*

Estimated Marginal Means

Grand Mean			
Dependent Variable: play			
Mean	Std. Error	95% Confidence Interval	
		Lower Bound	Upper Bound
4.620	.235	4.150	5.091

Descriptive Statistics - The results of the test showed comparisons among the marginal means for the three disabilities because (a) there is a significant disability main effect and a nonsignificant interaction and (b) the disability main effect has three levels. The researcher considered the appropriate methods to control for Type 1 error across the three groups. In addition, there were only three groups used in the LSD approach, which noted the Mean =4.6.

Homogeneous Subsets

	play				
	Disability status of the child	N	Subset		
			1	2	
Ryan-Einot-Gabriel-Welsch Range[a]	Physical Disability	20	3.20		
	Mental Retardation	20	3.65		
	Typically Developing	20		7.05	
	Sig.		.436	1.000	

Means for groups in homogeneous subsets are displayed.

Based on observed means.

The error term is Mean Square (Error) = 3.290.

a. Alpha = .05.

Table 5 *Homogeneous Subsets*

Inferential Statistics

Hypothesis 1. The results indicated that there is a significant difference in gender based on the disability status of the child, F (.436,) =, p= .436 (see Table 5 above). Therefore, the null is rejected, and the alternate hypothesis is accepted.

Hypothesis 2. The results indicated that there is no significant interaction between gender and disability status of the child and the amount of time fathers play with them, $F(1, 54) = .23$, $p = 63$. Therefore, the null hypothesis that states there is no significant interaction between gender and disability status of the child and the amount of time fathers play with them is accepted.

Hypothesis 3. The results indicate that there is no significant difference in the amount of time fathers spend with their children based on an interaction effect of disability by gender, F (2,

54) = .65, p = .53

Tests of Between-Subjects Effects						
Dependent Variable: play						
Source	Type III Sum of Squares	df	Mean Square	F	Sig.	Partial Eta Squared
Corrected Model	182.278ª	5	36.456	11.081	.000	.506
Intercept	1276.571	1	1276.571	388.025	.000	.878
disable	178.579	2	89.289	27.140	.000	.501
gender	.763	1	.763	.232	.632	.004
disable * gender	4.294	2	2.147	.653	.525	.024
Error	177.656	54	3.290			
Total	1648.000	60				
Corrected Total	359.933	59				
a. R Squared = .506 (Adjusted R Squared = .461)						

Table 6

Two-Way ANOVA: *Test of Between-Subject Effects* (Above)

Examination of the post hoc test indicated that fathers of typically developing children spent 3.85 more minutes playing with their children than fathers of children with a physical disability p =.>.001 and .3.40 more minutes playing with their children than fathers of children with some form of mental retardation p= >.001 (see Table 5).

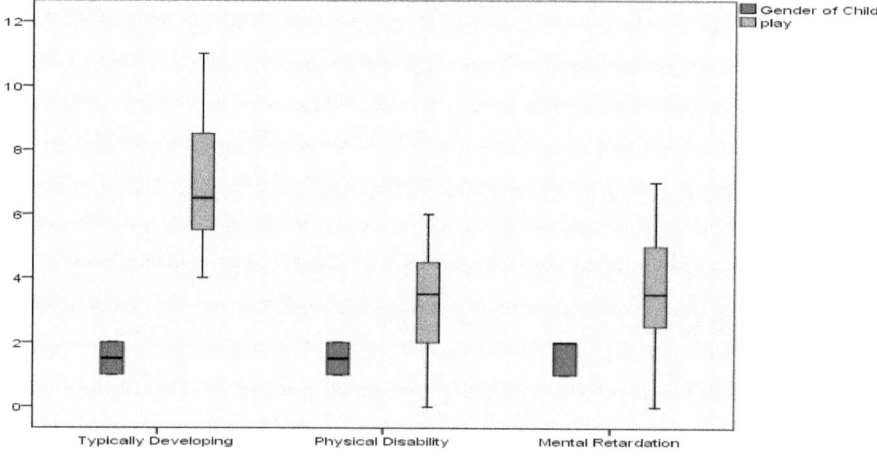

Boxplot: *Disability Status of the Child*

The purpose of this section was to determine how much time fathers of children with a disability played with their children. The researcher conducted a two-way ANOVA to evaluate differences among the groups, according to gender and disability status of the child, in the amount of time fathers spent playing with their children. The results in Hypothesis 1 indicated that there was a significant difference in gender based on the disability status of the child and the null hypothesis was rejected, and the alternate hypothesis was accepted.

The results from Hypothesis 2 indicated that there is no significant interaction between gender and disability status of the child and the amount of time fathers play with them. Therefore the null was not rejected. The results also indicated that there is no significant difference in the amount of time fathers spend with their children based on an interaction effect by disability by gender, thus hypotheses #3 was not rejected.

Recommendation: Further study is needed to determine if the age of the fathers and the age of the child with a disability contributes to the amount of time spent playing with their children.

Chapter 6: Data Interpretation Practicum One-Simple *t*-Test vs. ANOVA

A One-sample *t*-test evaluates whether the population mean on a test variable is different from a constant, called a test value by SPSS (p.146). Each case must have a score on one variable, the test variable. A major reason for selecting a One-sample *t*-test is choosing the test value. The test value typically represents a neutral point. Individuals who score higher than the neutral point are given one label, and those who score lower are given a different label (Green and Salkind, 2014). Those who fall exactly on the neutral point are given neither label.

For a one-way analysis of variance (one-way ANOVA), each individual, or case must have scores on two variables: a factor and a dependent variable. The factor divides individuals into two or more groups or levels, whereas the dependent variable differentiates individuals on a quantitative dimension. The AVONA *F* test evaluates whether the population means on the dependent variable differ across the levels of the factor (Green and Salkind, 2014 p.163). Each case in SPSS data file used to conduct a one-way ANOVA contains a factor that divides participants into groups and one quantitative dependent variable.

For this test, I opted to use the One-Simple *t* Test. The reason for my selection was that the result of the one-sample t test computes a mean and a standard deviation for the test variable. The purpose of this exercise was to determine does the mean change among the variables. Another reason for choosing the one-simple *t* test was it also reports the mean difference value, which is the difference between the mean of the test variable and the hypothesized value.

Purpose of the Test

From the week three assignment the purpose of the study was to determine if John's Involvement *Technique* for a new method was effective or not in teaching algebra to first graders. John randomly sampled six first graders from all the first graders within the Lawrence City School System. He proceeded to teach each student individually using the new method. Next, the six students completed an eight-item algebra test. The results from that test indicated that John's new method was not effective. However, to extend the study, Dana collected data from 20 college students on their emotional responses to classical music. Students listened to two 30-second segments from "The Collection from the Best of Classical Music". After listening to a segment, students rated it on a scale from 1 to 10, with 1 indicating "Makes me very sad" and 10 indicating, "Makes me very happy". Dana computes a total score (hap_sad) for each student by summing the student's two ratings. Dana conducts a one-sample *t* test to evaluate whether classical music makes students sad or happy.

Data Set Selected for this Test

The data set selected for this exercise is from Lesson 22 Exercise File 2 on the web at http://www.pearsonhighered.com/greensalkindSPSS. The test was conducted using the following steps click ANALYZE, select Compare Means, and then click One-Sample T Test.

Research Question

Does the mean change in the number of students indicating that classical music "makes me very sad from the students indicating that it "makes me happy?"

Hypotheses

H1$_0$ A mean difference does not exist among the number of students indicating classical music "makes me very sad from the students indicating that it "makes me happy.

H1$_A$ A mean difference does exist among the number of students indicating that classical music "makes me very sad from the students indicating it "makes me happy.

One-Sample Statistics				
	N	Mean	Std. Deviation	Std. Error Mean
hap_sad	20	8.75	4.734	1.058

Table 1 *One-Sample Statistics*

One-Sample Test						
				Test Value = 0		
	t	df	Sig. (2-tailed)	Mean Difference	95% Confidence Interval of the Difference	
					Lower	Upper
hap_sad	8.267	19	.000	8.750	6.53	10.97

Table 2 *One-Sample t Test*

Descriptive Statistics

A one-sample *t* test indicated that the mean on the emotional response scale ranging from 2 = very sad for both segments to 20 = very happy for both segments differed significantly from 11, the midpoint on the summed emotional response scale, *t=*

(19) = -2.13, p = .047. The sample mean and the standard deviation on the emotional response scores was 8.75 and 4.73. The 95% confidence interval for the emotional response mean ranged from 6.53 to 10.97. A d of -.48 indicated a medium effect size.

Inferential Statistics

The results supported the conclusion that classical music tends to make college students sad rather than happy t (19) = -2.13, p = .47 (see Table 1 and 2 above). The purpose of the test was to determine if a one-sample t test could evaluate whether classical music makes students sad or happy. Dana collected data from 20 college students on their emotional responses to classical music. Students listened to two 30-second segments from "The Collection from the Best of Classical Music". After listening to a segment, student rated it on a scale from 1 to 10, with 1 indicating "Makes me very sad" and 10 indicating, "Makes me very happy." Dana computes a total score (hap_sad) for each student by summing the student's two ratings. The results indicated that classical music does make college students sad rather than happy. Therefore, the null hypothesis "A mean difference does not exist among the number of students indicating classical music "makes me very sad from the students indicating that it "makes me happy" was rejected. And the Alternate hypothesis "A mean difference does exist among the number of students indicating that classical music "makes me very sad from the students indicating it "makes me happy" was accepted.

Recommendation: Do not play classical music to the 20 college students to evoke an emotional response that supports the happy emotion. Play music with an upbeat and faster tempo with happy lyrics to evoke the happy emotion.

Chapter 7: Measures and Scales

Item Analysis Using the Reliability Procedure - The methods used in the Reliability Analysis procedure assume that scale scores will be computed by summing item scores (Green and Salkind, 2014). An important thing to understand about Item Analysis using the Reliability Procedure is that after transforming items appropriately to create a meaningful total score for a scale, a correlation is computed between each item on the scale and the total score, excluding the item of interest from the total score. The reliability procedure can be used to determine the correlation of an item with its own corrected total scale scores. In addition, the Bivariate Correlation procedure is used to determine the correlation between item scores and total scores for other dimensions (Green and Salkind, 2014 p. 303). What is vital to remember is when making decisions about keeping or omitting items, the researcher must consider that content of the items and not just the magnitudes of the correlation coefficients. When using multiple constructs coefficient alphas must be computed to obtain internal consistency estimates of reliability for two coping scales as suggested by Green and Salkind, 2014.

What considerations must be made to ensure that the scale and test examples are reliable and valid for another population?

To ensure the scale and test examples are reliable and valid for another population a Kruskal-Wallis and the median tests evaluates whether the population medians on a dependent variable are the same across all levels of a factor. In addition, to compare the results to ensure validity, use the one-way ANOVA and the One-way ANCOVA to analyze the same data (Green and Salkind, 2014 p. 345). One assumption for the Kruskal-

Wallis test is if the population distributions differ on characteristics other than their medians, the Mann-Whitney test does not evaluate whether the medians differ among population, but whether the distributions themselves differ. Moreover, problems can arise with the Kruskal-Wallis test if there is not a variety of scores on the measure of interest and the ties produced in the ranked scores.

The article selected for this test was *"A study of the psychometric properties of the Beck Depression Inventory-II, the Montgomery and Åsberg Depression Rating Scale, and the Hospital Anxiety and Depression Scale in a sample from a healthy population"* which contained an example of a test and an example of a scale. The typical population was participants with no psychometric issues. The researchers used a selected sample from a healthy population (Kjaergaard, 2014). Participants answered two questionnaires and were interviewed with a structured clinical interview for diagnostic and statistical manual of mental disorders.

Three scales including depression sub-scale had a high area under the receiver operating characteristic curve and internal consistency was high for all scales (Kjaergaard, 2014). The results from the study indicated that depression scales in a healthy population were limited (Kjaergaard, 2014). The researcher found that the two screening instruments used for the study were acceptable (reliable) and supported valid results.

Chapter 8: Discriminant Analysis

Understanding discriminant analysis entails knowing that one or more linear combinations of quantitative predictors created are called discriminant functions (Green and Salkind, 2014). The number of possible discriminant functions for an analysis with N_g groups and p quantitative variables is either (N_g -1) or p, whichever is smaller. In addition, discriminant functions may be extracted that maximize the differences amongst groups, but always with a constraint that they are uncorrelated with all previously extracted functions as suggested by Green and Salkind, 2014.

I classified college professors into two groups, research scientists, and teaching moguls. Scores were obtained on four variables from 50 college professors, the number of publications in last two years, amount of grant funding generated in last five years, mean teaching evaluation score for the last three semesters, and the number of student committees served on during last five years. The researcher then had three university administrators evaluate all 50 professors as one of two types, research scientists, and teaching moguls. The SPSS data file had 50 cases and 5 variables. The five variables are the four predictors and a grouping variable distinguishing research scientists and teaching moguls based on the judgements of the university administrators. The researcher conducted a discriminant analysis to distinguish professors who are research scientists from professors who were teaching moguls. From the output, the researcher identified the following: (a) research scientist group mean from the number of publications, (b) univariate ANOVA F value for grant money, (c) X_2 associated with the discriminant function. In addition, identified the percentage of research scientists are correctly classified, and what overall percentage of professors correctly classified as teaching mogul and research scientists.

Reason for selecting Discriminant Analysis

The reason for selecting discriminant analysis was that it could be used to classify individuals into groups based on one or more measures. In addition, distinguish groups based on linear combinations of measures and possibly obtain a significant F test with a MANOVA. For discriminant analysis, each case must have a score or scores on one or more quantitative variable as described by Green and Salkind, 2014. Moreover, must have a value on a classification variable that indicates group membership.

Data Set Selected for this Test

The data set selected for this exercise is from Lesson 35 Exercise File 1 on the web at http://www.pearsonhighered.com/greensalkindSPSS. The test was conducted using the following steps click ANALYZE, Classify, and selecting Discriminant.

Research Question

Can the individuals in the three job-performance groups be correctly classified into three categories based on the scores on the four-predictor variables?

Hypotheses

H1$_0$ A significant relationship does not exist between classifying the three job-performance groups based on scores of the four-predictor variables.

H1$_A$ A significant relationship does exist between classifying the three job-performance group based on scores of the four-predictor variables.

GROUP STATISTICS					
TYPE OF PROFESSOR		Mean	Std. Deviation	Valid N (listwise) Unweighted	Weighted
TEACHING MOGUL	Number of publications in last 2 years	3.4800	.82260	25	25.000

	Grant funding (in $10000) over the last 5 years	4.5471	3.17875	25	25.000
	Mean teaching rating for last 3 semesters	3.5122	.42025	25	25.000
	Number of committees served on during last 5 years	3.4800	2.23830	25	25.000
TOTAL	Number of publications in last 2 years	3.4800	.82260	25	25.000
	Grant funding (in $10000) over the last 5 years	4.5471	3.17875	25	25.000
	Mean teaching rating for last 3 semesters	3.5122	.42025	25	25.000
	Number of committees served on during last 5 years	3.4800	2.23830	25	25.000

Table 1-*Group Statistics*

POOLED WITHIN-GROUPS MATRICES

		Number of publications in last 2 years	Grant funding (in $10000) over the last 5 years	Mean teaching rating for last 3 semesters	Number of committees served on during last 5 years
CORRELATION	Number of publications in last 2 years	1.000	-.112	-.431	.164
	Grant funding (in $10000) over the last 5 years	-.112	1.000	.051	.651
	Mean teaching rating for last 3 semesters	-.431	.051	1.000	-.236
	Number of committees served on during last 5 years	.164	.651	-.236	1.000

Table 2 – *Pooled Within Groups Matrices*

Descriptive Statistics

A discriminant analysis test was conducted and the results indicated that the mean $= 2.92$, $F(1, 48) = .05$, $p = .83$, $X_2 = (4, N = 50) = 22.85$. Eighty percent of the research scientists were classified correctly, and 84% of the total group of professors was classified accurately. Using leave-one-out classification, 72% of the research scientists were classified correctly, and 78% of the total group of professors was classified accurately. The results were obtained based on prior probabilities computed from group sizes.

In addition, a discriminant analysis was conducted to determine whether several academic factors, number of publication, amount of grant funding, teaching evaluation scores, and number of student committees, predict if professors are research scientists or teaching moguls. Wilk's lambda was significant, $A = .61$, $X2 (4, N = 50) = 22.85$, $p < .01$, indicated differences on the four academic factors between the two professor groups. Tables 1 and 2 outlined the within-group correlations and the standardized weights between the academic factors and the discriminant function. Both the correlations and the standardized weights, the teaching evaluation scores and the number of publications have strong relationship with the discriminant function.

Inferential Statistics

Professors were classified based on the four academic factors. The assumption was that equality of the covariance matrices and determined prior probabilities from the sample group sizes. Eighty-four percent of the professors were correctly classified as teaching moguls and research scientists. To estimate how well the classification method would predict in future samples, the researcher conducted a leave-one-out analysis. The results indicated that 78% of professors were classified accurately.

The purpose of the test was to classify college professors into two groups, research scientists, and teaching moguls. In addition, obtain scores on four variables from 50 college professors, the number of publications in last two years, amount of grant funding generated in last five years, mean teaching evaluation score for the last three semesters, and the number of student committees served on during last five years. The results indicated the discriminant function appeared to represent an ability to acquire and impart knowledge. Individuals in the teaching group have, on the average, higher scores on this function. The results indicated that 78% of professors were classified accurately. Therefore, the null **H1₀** A significant relationship does not exist between classifying the three job-performance groups based on scores of the four-predictor variables was rejected. And the Alternate **H1ₐ** A significant relationship does exist between classifying three job-performance group based on scores of the four-predictor variables is accepted.

Chapter 9: SPSS Exercises - Chi Square Test and Nonparametric Procedures

One-Sample Chi Square Test

The one-sample chi-square test evaluates whether the proportions of individuals who fall into categories of a variable are equal to hypothesized values (Green and Salkind, 2014). It is possible for the variable to have two or more categories. The one-sample chi-square test yields significance if the sample proportions for the categories differ from the hypothesized proportions and if the sample size is large.

Purpose of the Exercises

The purpose of the tests were to evaluate whether the method of cooking potato chips affects the taste of the chips. The researcher had 48 individuals volunteer to participate in the potato chip study. Each participant-tasted chips cooked using three different methods: fried in animal fat (chip =1), fried in canola oil (chip =2), and baked (chip =3). Individuals were instructed to indicate which type of potato chips they preferred: chip type 1, chip type 2, or chip type 3. The researcher hypothesized that individuals would prefer potato chips that were fried in canola oil over those that were fried in animal fat or baked. The test weighted the number of cases, and conducted a one-sample chi-square test to evaluate whether the cooking method affected taste. From the output, the following as identified: the frequency for potato chips fried in canola oil, the p value, X_2 value, the expected frequencies for the three categories of potato chips.

Data Set for this Test

The data set selected for this exercise was from Lesson 40 Exercise File 1. on the web at http://www.pearsonhighered.com/greensalkindSPSS. The test was conducted using the following steps click ANALYZE, click Nonparametric Test, legacy Dialogs, and then select Chi-Square.

Research Question

Do individuals prefer potato chips that are fried in canola oil over those that are fried in animal fat or baked?

Hypotheses

H1₀ A significant difference does not exist between individuals that prefer fried potato chips in canola oil over those that are fried in animal fat or baked.

H1ₐ A significant difference does exist between individuals that prefer fried potato chips in canola oil over those that are fried in animal fat or baked.

Method of cooking potato chips			
	Observed N	Expected N	Residual
Fried in animal fat	7	16.0	-9.0
Fried in Canola oil	33	16.0	17.0
Baked	8	16.0	-8.0
Total	48		

Table 1-*Chi-Square Test Method of cooking potatoes chips*

Descriptive Statistics

A One-Sample Chi-Square test was conducted and the results indicated that the frequency was 33, the p .0, X_2 (2, $N = 48$) = 27.12. The expected frequency for each potato chip category was 16 which was significant. Therefore, the null **H1₀** A significant difference does not exist between individuals that prefer fried potato chips in canola oil over those that are fried in animal fat or baked was rejected.

Number who preferred each type of chip			
	Observed N	Expected N	Residual
7	7	16.0	-9.0
8	8	16.0	-8.0
33	33	16.0	17.0
Total	48		

Table 2 – *Number who preferred each type of chip*

Inferential Statistics

A One-Sample Chi-Square test was conducted to assess whether potato chips tasted better when fried in canola oil as opposed to fried in animal fat or baked. The results of the test were significant, X_2 (2, $N = 48$) $= 27.12$, $p < .01$. The test was significant because the observed frequency of chips fried in canola oil of 33 was much greater than the expected frequency of 16. In addition, while the observed frequencies of chips fried in animal fat or baked (n = 7 and $n = 8$), were less than the expected frequency of 16.

	Test Statistics	
	Method of cooking potato chips	Number who preferred each type of chip
Chi-Square	27.125[a]	27.125[a]
df	2	2
Asymp. Sig.	.000	.000
a. 0 cells (0.0%) have expected frequencies less than 5. The minimum expected cell frequency is 16.0.		

Table 3 – *Test Statistics*

A follow-up analysis was conducted to evaluate whether the proportion of individuals who preferred chips fried in canola oil and the proportion of individuals who prefer chips fried in animal fat or baked differ significantly from chance values of .33 and .67. The results of the test were significant, X_2 (1, $N = 48$) $= 27.09$, $p < .01$, indicated that individuals prefer potato chips fried in canola oil rather than in animal fat or baked. Therefore, the null **H1o** A significant difference does not exist between individuals that prefer fried potato chips in canola oil over those that are fried in animal fat or baked was rejected.

Nonparametric Procedures Exercises 1-4 (The Mann-Whitney U Test)

The Mann Whitney U test evaluates whether the medians on a test variable differ significantly between two groups (Green and Salkind, 2014). According to Green and Salkind (2014) in an SPSS data file, each case must have scores on two variables, the grouping variable, and the test variable (p. 338). The grouping variable divides cases into two groups or categories, and the test variable assesses individuals on a variable with at least an ordinal scale. Understanding the Mann-Whitney U Test (Nonparametric Procedures) entails first describing what data is analyzed with the test. Next, the scores on the test variable are converted to ranks, ignoring group membership. Because analyses for the Mann-Whitney U test are conducted on ranked scores, the distributions of the test variable for the two populations do not have to be of any particular form. However, these distributions should be continuous and have identical forms according to Green and Salkind, 2014, p. 338.

Purpose of the Test

The researcher wishes to test the hypothesis that overweight individuals tend to eat faster than normal weight individuals do. To test this hypothesis, the researcher had two assistants sit in a McDonald's restaurant and identify individuals who ordered at lunchtime the Big Mac special that contained large fries and a large Coke. The Big Mackers, as the assistants called this group were classified as overweight, normal weight, or neither overweight nor normal weight. The assistants identified 10 overweight Big Mackers and 30 normal weight Big Mackers (individuals who were neither overweight nor normal weight were disregarded). The assistants recorded the amount of time it took for the individuals in two groups to complete their Big Mac special meals. One variable was weighted with two levels, overweight (=1) and Normal weight (= 2). The second variable is timed in seconds.

The results from the Mann-Whitney U test identified the following: p value, z value corrected for ties, Mean rank for normal weight individuals. In addition, an independent-samples t test was conducted to compare the p value, the Mann-Whitney U test, and the independent-samples t test.

Data Set for this Test

The data set selected for this exercise is from Lesson 42 Exercise File 1 on the web at http://www.pearsonhighered.com/greensalkindSPSS. The test was conducted using the following steps click ANALYZE, select Nonparametric Test, click Legacy Dialogs, and then select 2 Independent Samples.

Research Question

Do overweight individuals tend to eat faster than normal weight individuals do?

Hypotheses

$H1_0$ There is no significant difference that overweight individuals tend to eat faster than normal weight individuals.

$H1_A$ There is significant difference that overweight individuals tend to eat faster than normal weight individuals.

Ranks				
	weight	N	Mean Rank	Sum of Ranks
Time in Seconds	overweight	10	8.30	83.00
	normal weight	30	24.57	737.00
	Total	40		

Table 1- *Ranks*

Descriptive Statistics

A Mann-Whitney U test was conducted the results indicated that $p < .01$, $z = -3.81$, and the Mean rank = 24.57. The p value for an independent-samples t test was the same as the p value obtained for the Mann-Whitney U test.

Test Statistics[a]	
	Time in Seconds
Mann-Whitney U	28.000
Wilcoxon W	83.000
Z	-3.811
Asymp. Sig. (2-tailed)	.000
Exact Sig. [2*(1-tailed Sig.)]	.000[b]
a. Grouping Variable: weight	
b. Not corrected for ties.	

Table 2 – *Test Statistics*

Case Processing Summary								
	weight	Cases						
		Valid		Missing		Total		
		N	Percent	N	Percent	N	Percent	
Time in Seconds	overweight	10	100.0%	0	0.0%	10	100.0%	
	normal weight	30	100.0%	0	0.0%	30	100.0%	

Table 3- *Weight and Time in Seconds*

Inferential Statistics

A Mann-Whitney U test was conducted to evaluate the hypothesis that overweight individuals would eat Big Mac meals faster than normal weight individuals would. The results of the test were significant, $z = -3.81$, $p < .01$, with the overweight individuals having a mean rank eating time of 8.30 and normal weight individuals having a mean rank of 24.57.

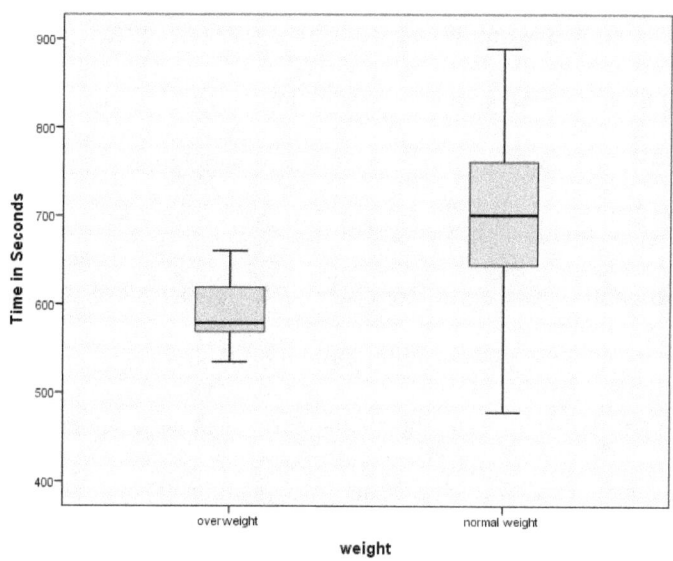

Figure 1 – Shows the distributions of the time spent eating a Big Mac meal for overweight and normal-weight individuals.

The purpose of this test was to determine whether overweight individuals tend to eat faster than normal weight individuals do. The researcher had two assistants sit in a McDonald's restaurant and identify individuals who ordered at lunchtime the Big Mac special that contained large fries and a large Coke. The assistants recorded the amount of time it took for the individuals in two groups to complete their Big Mac special meals. One variable was weighted with two levels, overweight (=1) and Normal weight (= 2). The second variable is time in seconds.

A Mann-Whitney U test was conducted to evaluate the hypothesis that overweight individuals would eat Big Mac meals faster than normal weight individuals would. The results of the test were significant, $z = -3.81$, $p < .01$, with the overweight individuals having a mean rank eating time of 8.30 and normal weight individuals having a mean rank of 24.57. Therefore, the null **H1o** There is no significant difference that overweight individuals tend to eat faster than normal weight individuals was rejected. In addition, the alternate **H1A** There is significant difference that overweight individuals tend to eat faster than normal weight individuals was accepted.

Nonparametric Procedures Exercises 1-5 K Independent-Samples Test

The Kruskal-Wallis and the Median Test

Both the Kruskal-Wallis and the median tests evaluate whether the population medians on a dependent variable are the same across all levels of a factor (Green and Salkind, 2014). For the Kruskal-Wallis and the median tests using the K independent samples procedure, cases must have scores on an independent or grouping variable and on a dependent or test variable. To understand how Kruskal-Wallsi and median test evaluate differences in medians among groups, first describe what data is analyzed for each test.

Purpose of the Test

The purpose of the test was to determine whether blonde-haired people, brunets, and redheads differ in their extroversion. The researcher randomly samples 18 mean from the local college campus: six blonde-haired people, six brunets, and six redheads. Next, administered a measure of social extroversion to each individual. The results from the Kruskal-Wallis test showed the relationship between hair color and social extroversion, and the effect size for the overall effect of hair color on extroversion.

Data Set for this Test

The data set selected for this exercise is from Lesson 43 Exercise File 1 on the web at http://www.pearsonhighered.com/greensalkindSPSS. The test was conducted using the following steps click DATA, select Cases, Next click All Cases, then select OK. The select ANALYZE, Nonparametric, click K Independent Samples.

Research Question

What is the significant difference between the levels of extroversion by hair color?

Hypotheses

$H1_0$ (Null) There is no significant difference in level of extroversion by hair color.

$H1_A$ (Alternate) There is a significant difference in level of extroversion by hair color.

Ranks			
	Hair Color	N	Mean Rank
Social Extroversion	Blond	6	12.75
	Brunet	6	10.25
	Redhead	6	5.50
	Total	18	

Table 1- *Kruskal-Wallis Test (Ranks)*

Test Statistics[a,b]	
	Social Extroversion
Chi-Square	5.963
df	2
Asymp. Sig.	.051
a. Kruskal Wallis Test	

b. Grouping Variable: Hair
Color

Table 2- *Kruskal-Wallis Test Statistics*

Descriptive Statistics

 A Kruskal-Wallis Test was conducted and the results indicated that follow-up test may not be conducted because the overall test is not significant at the .05 level, X_2 (2, N = 18) = 5.96, p = .051. In addition, the test, which was corrected for tied ranks, was not significant. The proportion of variability in the ranked extroversion scores accounted for by hair color variable was .35 indicated a strong relationship between hair color and extroversion in the sample.

Test Statistics[a]

	Social Extroversion
N	18
Median	3.00
Chi-Square	3.150[b]
df	2
Asymp. Sig.	.207

a. Grouping Variable: Hair Color

b. 6 cells (100.0%) have expected frequencies less than 5. The minimum expected cell frequency is 2.7.

Table 3- *Median Test Statistics*

Inferential Statistics

 The results from the Median Test conducted indicate the F (2, 15 = 3.51) for the group effect size. In addition, a Kruskal-Wallis test was conducted to evaluate differences in extroversion among men with three different hair colors: blonds, brunets, and redhead.

The test for tied ranks was not significant, X_2 (2, N = 18) = 5.96, p = .051.

Frequencies

		Hair Color		
		Blond	Brunet	Redhead
Social Extroversion	> Median	4	3	1
	<= Median	2	3	5

Table 4- *Median Frequencies*

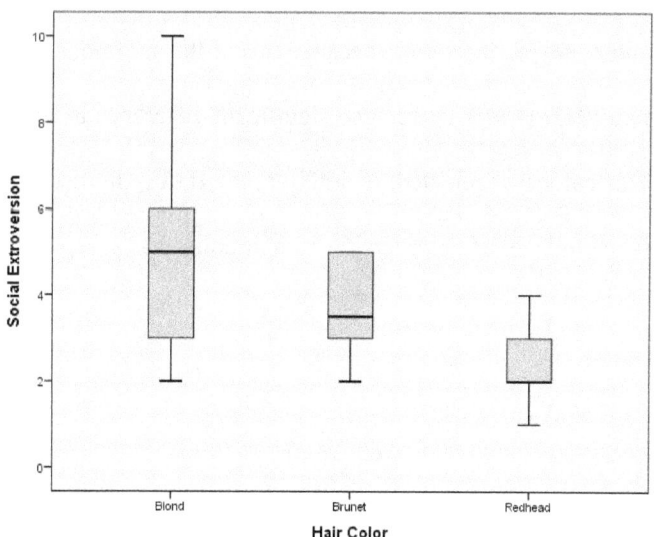

Table 5- *Boxplot*

Conclusion

The purpose of the test was to determine whether blonde-haired people, brunets,

and redheads differ in their extroversion. The researcher randomly samples 18 mean from the local college campus: six blonde-haired people, six brunets, and six redheads. The results from the Kruskal-Wallis Test indicated a strong relationship between hair color and extroversion in a male population. The results of the median test were significant. However, the p value may be inaccurate because two of the six frequencies are less than 5. Therefore, the null **H1$_0$** (Null) There is no significant difference in level of extroversion by hair color was rejected. In addition, the **H1$_A$** (Alternate) There is a significant difference in level of extroversion by hair color was accepted.

References

American Psychological Association. (2010). *Publication manual of the American Psychological Association* (6th ed.). Washington: Author.

Campbell, D. T., & Stanley, J. (2010). *Experimental and quasi-experimental designs for research* (Laureate Education Inc., custom ed.). Mason, OH: Cengage Learning.

Corner, P. D. (2002). An integrative model for teaching quantitative research design. *Journal of Management Education, 26*, 671–6 92. doi: 10.1177/1052562902238324

Creswell, J. W. (2013). *Qualitative inquiry & research design: Choosing among five approaches* (3rd ed.). Thousand Oaks, CA: Sage.

Creswell, J. W. (2013*). Research design: Qualitative, quantitative, and mixed methods approaches* (Laureate Education, Inc., custom ed.). Thousand Oaks, CA: Sage.

Green, S. B., & Salkind, N. J. (2014). *Using SPSS for Windows and Macintosh: Analyzing and understanding data* (7th ed.). Upper Saddle River, NJ: Pearson.

Kahn, W. A. (2013). Organizational crises and the disturbance of relational systems. *Academy of Management Review*, 377-396. doi:10.5465/amr.2011.0363

Kjærgaard, M., Arfwedson Wang, C. E., Waterloo, K., & Jorde, R. (2014). A study of the psychometric properties of the Beck Depression Inventory-II, the Montgomery and Ásberg Depression Rating Scale, and the hospital anxiety and depression scale in a sample from a healthy population. *Scandinavian Journal of Psychology, 55*(1), 83-89. doi:10.1111/sjop.12090

Mann, S. (2014). Human resources and emergency planning: Preparing local

governments for times of crisis. *Public Administration Quarterly*, *38*(2), 163-205.

Pearson Education. (2010). *Datasets to accompany* Using SPSS for Windows and

Macintosh *by Green and Salkind* [Data file]. Retrieved from

http://www.prenhall.com/greensalkind/GreenSalkind.zip

Pinto, A., Ribeiro, R. A., & Nunes, I. L. (2013). Ensuring the quality of occupational

safety risk assessment. *Risk Analysis: An International Journal*, *33*, 409-419.

doi:10.1111/j.1539-6924.2012.01898.x

Ruggiero, A., & Vos, M. (2013). Terrorism Communication: Characteristics and

Emerging Perspectives in the Scientific Literature 2002-2011. *Journal of

Contingencies & Crisis Management*, *21*(3), 153-166. doi:10.1111/1468-

5973.12022

United States Department of Labor (2014). *Occupational Safety & Health

Administration.* Retrieved from United States Department of Labor

https://www.osha.gov

Additional Material and Contact Information

Dr. Enid A. Thompson has also authored the following books:

- I'm Coming For You

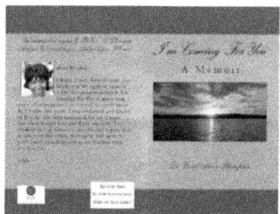

- Managing Effective Communication After a Crisis

- Organizational Change and Employee Retention: Strange Bedfellows

- Sustainable Solutions For a Successful Business

Her new book entitled "Let's Get Busy" will be released early 2018. "Let's Get Busy" is

the sequel in the New Earth Series from Dr. Enid as a follow-up to "What Now?" This

book is an in-depth look how each of us has a role in creating the new systems we all

desire in the educational and legislative branch of our country. Interested in booking Dr.

Thompson as a speaker, email her team at dr.enid@yahoo.com or by calling Guide

Consultants (813) 563-2076. Dr. Enid lives in Wesley Chapel, Florida with her husband

James. They have two adult children and two grandchildren. For more information about

Dr. Enid and her work go to www.consultwithdrenid.com

The New Earth Series Presents

Quantitative Decision-Making for Business Analysis

By

Dr. Enid Alane Thompson

Published by CreateSpace Self-Publishing (LLC), an Amazon Company, and Kindle

Direct Publishing (LLC) Copyright of Book is held by the Author.

2016

www.ingramcontent.com/pod-product-compliance
Lightning Source LLC
Chambersburg PA
CBHW061215180526
45170CB00003B/1015